The Homeless

Distinguishing Between Fact and Opinion

Curriculum Consultant: JoAnne Buggey, Ph.D.
College of Education, University of Minnesota

By Teresa O'Neill

Greenhaven Press, Inc.
Post Office Box 289009
San Diego, CA 92198–0009

Titles in the opposing viewpoints juniors series:

AIDS
Alcohol
Animal Rights
Death Penalty
Drugs and Sports
The Environment
Gun Control
The Homeless
Immigration
Nuclear Power

The Palestinian Conflict
Patriotism
Poverty
Prisons
Smoking
Television
Toxic Wastes
The U.S. Constitution
Working Mothers
Zoos

Cover photo: 1989 O'Brien and Mayor Photography/FPG International

Library of Congress Cataloging-in-Publication Data

O'Neill, Terry, 1944–
    The homeless: distinguishing between fact and opinion / by Teresa
O'Neill; curriculum consultant, JoAnne Buggey.
        p. cm. — (Opposing viewpoints juniors)
    Summary: Readers learn to apply critical thinking skills to
distinguish between facts and opinions in arguments about society's
attitude toward the homeless and the best way to help them.
    ISBN 0-89908-605-5
    1. Homelessness—United States—Juvenile literature.   2. Critical
thinking—Juvenile literature.   [1. Homelessness.   2. Homeless
persons.]   I. Buggey, JoAnne.   II. Title.   III. Series.
    HV4505.055 1990
    362.5′0973—dc20   90-45283

CONTENTS

An Introduction to Opposing Viewpoints

When people disagree, it is hard to figure out who is right. You may decide one person is right just because the person is your friend or relative. But this is not a very good reason to agree or disagree with someone. It is better if you try to understand why these people disagree. On what main points do the two people disagree? Read or listen to each person's argument carefully. Separate the facts and opinions that each person presents. Finally, decide which argument best matches what you think. This process, examining an argument without emotion, is part of what critical thinking is all about.

This is not easy. Many things make it hard to understand and form opinions. People's values, age, and experience all influence the way they think. This is why learning to read and think critically is an invaluable skill. Opposing Viewpoints Juniors books will help

you learn and practice skills to improve your ability to read critically. By reading opposing views on an issue, you will become familiar with methods people use to attempt to convince you that their point of view is right. And you will learn to separate the authors' opinions from the facts they present.

Each Opposing Viewpoints Juniors book focuses on one critical thinking skill that will help you judge the views presented. Some of these skills are telling fact from opinion, recognizing propaganda techniques, and locating and analyzing the main idea. These skills will allow you to examine opposing viewpoints more easily. Each viewpoint is paraphrased from the original to make it easier to read. The viewpoints are placed in a running debate and are always placed with the pro view first.

What Is the Difference Between Fact and Opinion?

In this Opposing Viewpoints Juniors book you will be asked to identify and study statements of fact and statements of opinion. A fact is a statement that can be proved true. Here are some examples of factual statements: "The Statue of Liberty was dedicated in 1886 in New York," "Dinosaurs are extinct," and "George Washington was the first U.S. president." It is a fairly easy thing to prove these facts true. For instance, a historian in the year 3000 might need to prove when the Statue of Liberty was dedicated. One way she might do this is to check in the Hall of Records in New York. She would try to find a source to verify the date. Sometimes it is harder to prove facts true. And some ideas that are stated as facts may not be. In this book you will be asked to question facts presented in the viewpoints and be given some ways in which you might go about proving them.

Statements of opinion cannot be proved. An opinion is a statement that expresses how a person feels about something or what a person thinks is true. Remember the facts we mentioned? They can easily be changed into statements of opinion. For example, "Dinosaurs became extinct because a huge meteor hit the Earth," "George Washington was the best president the United States ever had," and "Rebuilding the Statue of Liberty was a waste of money," are all statements of opinion. They express what one person believes to be true. Opinions are not better than facts. They are different. Opinions are based on many things, including religious, social, moral, and family values. Opinions can also be based on medical and scientific facts. For instance, many scientists have made intelligent guesses about other planets based on what they know is true about Earth. The only way these scientists would know their opinions were right is if they were able to visit other planets and test their guesses. Until their guesses are proved, then, they remain opinions. Some people have opinions that we do not like, or with which we disagree. That does not always make their opinions wrong, or right. There is room in our world for many different opinions.

When you read differing views on any issue, it is very important to know when people are using facts and when they are using opinions in an argument. When writers use facts, it makes their argument more believable and easier to prove. The more facts the author has, the more the reader can tell that the writer's opinion is based on something other than personal feelings.

Authors that base their arguments mostly on their own opinions, then, are impossible to prove factually true.

This does not mean that these types of argument are not as meaningful. It means that you, as the reader, must decide whether or not you agree or disagree based on personal reasons, not factual ones.

We asked two students to give their opinions on the homeless issue. Examine the following viewpoints. Look for facts and opinions in their arguments.

I think we should help the homeless.

I'm lucky. I live in a pretty nice neighborhood. But not everyone is so lucky. When I walk to school, I see homeless people who live in our neighborhood. Well, they don't exactly *live* here. They stay in our park at night. Sometimes I also see squashed cardboard boxes in the glass booth around our bank machine. My mom says that homeless people use the cardboard to keep warm when they sleep in the booth. I think this is terrible. There is no reason for people to have to live like this in our country. There are empty buildings in many areas of our city. Instead of standing abandoned and useless, why can't they be made into homes for the homeless? If all of us would give up just a little bit, we could help these people. We could volunteer our time and labor and collect donations of money and materials from big companies. Then we could fix up these old buildings and get these poor people off the street.

> ## I think the homeless should help themselves.

I hate it when I go downtown and see homeless people sitting around on park benches and in the library. Most of them look dirty and smell like liquor. A lot of them beg for money. It's disgusting. Some of the news stories say there are homeless families. The parents and children spend nights in cars and under bridges. But I don't believe this. The homeless people I see are almost all adult men. They look healthy. Why don't they get jobs? I learned in school about the welfare system and about organizations like the Salvation Army and Catholic Charities that have shelters and give help to these people. But it seems the homeless prefer to hang around the streets and annoy regular people who have jobs. I think if they wanted to, most homeless people could help themselves. They are homeless because they are too lazy to be responsible.

If someone wanted to know which side you were on, who would you agree with? Why?

ANALYZING THE
SAMPLE VIEWPOINTS

Louis and Camille have very different opinions about homeless people. Both of them use examples of fact and opinion in their arguments.

Louis:

FACTS	OPINIONS
I see homeless people in our neighborhood.	I'm lucky.
They stay in our park.	I think this is terrible.
There are empty buildings in our city.	There is no reason for people to live like this.

Camille:

FACTS	OPINIONS
News stories say there are homeless families.	I hate it when I see homeless people downtown.
I learned in school about the welfare system.	Most homeless people look healthy.
Organizations like the Salvation Army have shelters for the homeless.	I think most homeless people could help themselves.

In this sample, Louis and Camille both have an equal number of facts and opinions. Louis's facts are based on personal experience. Camille's facts, on the other hand, are based on information from other sources—school, the newspaper, and so forth. Both Louis and Camille think they are right about homeless people. What conclusions do you come to from this sample? Why? Think of two facts you know and two opinions you have about the homeless.

As you continue to read the viewpoints in this book, try keeping a tally like the one above to compare the authors' arguments.

PREFACE: Is Homelessness a Serious Problem?

For the past few years, the homeless have been the focus of numerous stories on television, in newspapers, and in news magazines. But is the problem of homelessness as serious as some articles would have us believe? The next two viewpoints debate this question. Each author looks at facts and statistics about the homeless, but each draws a very different conclusion.

When reading these two viewpoints, use your skills to find the facts and opinions each author presents. Which case is more strongly based on fact, or are they equally factual?

Editor's Note: The author of the following viewpoint takes the stand that homelessness is a very serious problem in the United States. She suggests several reasons for homelessness.

The first part of the first sentence is a factual statement. The second part tells the source of the fact. To determine if the statement is true, you would have to find out Snyder's source of information.

The United States has over three million homeless people, according to Mitch Snyder. Snyder was an advocate for the homeless. He and Mary Ellen Hombs wrote an article called "Sheltering the Homeless: An American Imperative." It was published in the November/December 1986 issue of *State Government: The Journal of State Affairs.* In it, the two authors say there are many reasons for homelessness. Some of them are the following:

- There is not enough affordable housing. In many cities, the poorer—and cheaper—areas have been "cleaned up." Cheap, rundown houses have been eliminated.
- Many people who are mentally or physically ill and should be in a hospital are out on the streets. But hospitals have to cut costs, and government programs will not pay enough to take care of these people for very long.
- The government has reduced its spending on social programs. This means that poor families are getting less help from programs like AFDC (Aid to Families with Dependent Children). Older and handicapped people are getting less help from Social Security. Even the food stamp program has been reduced.

One fact stated in this paragraph is that the government has reduced its spending on AFDC. You could check to see if this is true at the public library or in an article about the government's annual budget.

Don Wright/*The Miami News.* Reprinted with permission.

- Unemployment is too high. Certain areas depend heavily on jobs in one particular industry. If something goes wrong in that industry, there are no jobs. For example, when the auto industry began having bad problems, millions of people were put out of jobs.
- Many people, especially older people, are on "fixed incomes." This means that no matter what, they get the same amount of money each month from Social Security or other retirement plans. Each year living expenses go up: Food costs more; heat costs more; housing costs more.
- The breakup of families has led to greater poverty, especially of children, women, and old people. When a family breaks up, two households have to be supported on the same amount of money that formerly supported one.

Anyone who does not think homelessness is serious should take a walk or drive around their town at night. Almost every city has people that have no place to live. Many of these people are just like you and your neighbors except that they have had bad luck. Sometimes a family member gets sick and medical bills take all the family's money. They lose their home when they can no longer pay the bills for it. Sometimes the family has only one adult and that person cannot earn enough money to provide a home and food for the family. An adult who has a high school education or less can sometimes only get an unskilled job that may not pay enough to support a family. Sometimes even highly skilled and trained people cannot find a job for a very long time.

Do you think the second sentence in this paragraph is a fact or an opinion? Does your city have homeless people? Have you seen them?

Jonathan Kozol is a former teacher who has written several books about education and poor children. In *Rachel's Children,* he wrote, "[Homelessness] has grown into the common misery of millions." According to Kozol, in 1988 New York City had more than twenty-eight thousand homeless people in emergency shelters. Another forty thousand were unsheltered, wandering around the city. Kozol also says that 40 percent of the homeless people in America are children.

These statistics help prove what our eyes tell us: Homelessness is a very serious problem that our society must try to solve.

Is the author's conclusion a fact or an opinion?

Why is homelessness serious?

The author lists six reasons homelessness occurs. What are these reasons? Does the author use facts to prove these reasons are true?

Editor's Note: The author of the following viewpoint argues that homelessness is not nearly as serious as some people would have us believe. The author cites facts from various studies that show the number of homeless people is much lower than stated in Viewpoint 1.

The first paragraph states the author's viewpoint. Is it a fact or an opinion? How do you know?

Yes, there are homeless people in this country. But the homeless problem is not anywhere near as serious as some people say it is.

Advocates for the homeless say there are about three million homeless people in the United States. But they do not show how they came to this conclusion. It is very difficult to determine the exact number of homeless people. The truly homeless do not stay in one place for very long. They live on the streets or in their cars. They move from shelter to shelter. This is the reason that even careful studies by several organizations show very different numbers. Still, attempts are made to count them.

The National Academy of Sciences published an important book called *Homelessness, Health and Human Needs.* It discusses several respected studies of the homeless. None of them estimated a number anywhere close to three million. For example,

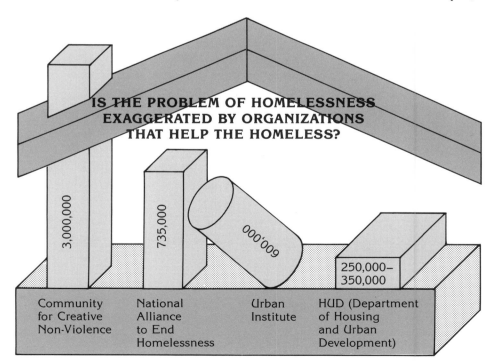

IS THE PROBLEM OF HOMELESSNESS EXAGGERATED BY ORGANIZATIONS THAT HELP THE HOMELESS?

Community for Creative Non-Violence	National Alliance to End Homelessness	Urban Institute	HUD (Department of Housing and Urban Development)
3,000,000	735,000	600,000	250,000–350,000

a study by the U.S. Department of Housing and Urban Development (HUD) determined that there are about 250,000 to 350,000 homeless people. A study by the National Alliance to End Homelessness determined that there are about 735,000 homeless people. The Urban Institute counted about 600,000 homeless. These numbers vary a lot because the numbers are estimates. Shelter managers, social workers, and others who work with the homeless report the numbers of people they serve. These workers are the people best qualified to determine the right numbers. The studies then use these numbers to come up with an approximate total. If these studies are right, homelessness affects only a very small part of our population—only about two people in one thousand. This means that the figure of 3 million homeless is false. Certain advocates of the homeless use it to advance their cause. They care more for their cause than for the truth.

Homeless advocates try to make us believe that millions of children and adults are suffering lives of horror, living on the streets, in parks, and under bridges. In truth, the few hundred thousand people who are homeless are almost all adults. They are almost all mentally ill or they have problems with alcohol and drugs. Some of them are people who cannot fit into society because of their problems. Many of these people could fit into society if they got some help. But it is against the law to force homeless mentally ill people into institutions. And the chemical abusers do not want help. They want to continue living with their drugs. Society cannot do much about people who feel like this.

Yes, society should try to help these people. But we should also try to keep the problem in perspective. Those who say homelessness is a more serious problem than it really is are lying to us. If we believe them, we will not work to solve really serious problems such as the national debt, poor schools, and crime.

All the studies list different numbers of homeless people. The numbers are all estimates. They are opinions based on information their originators thought was reasonable and factual.

The sentence beginning "But it is against the law. . ." is a factual statement. Discuss with your teacher or librarian how you could find out if it is true.

Do you think the sentence "And the chemical abusers do not want help" is a fact or an opinion? Why?

Is the homeless problem exaggerated?

The author argues that advocates for the homeless exaggerate the seriousness of the problem. How could you find out if homelessness is a serious problem in your community?

CRITICAL THINKING SKILL 1

Tallying the Facts and Opinions

After reading the first two viewpoints on homelessness, make a chart similar to the one made for Louis and Camille on page 8. List the facts and opinions each author gives to make her case. A chart is started for you below.

Viewpoint 1:

FACTS	OPINIONS
There are over three million homeless people.	Homelessness is a serious problem.

Viewpoint 2:

FACTS	OPINIONS
Homeless people are hard to count accurately.	The homeless problem is not serious.

Which article used more factual statements? Which do you think was the most convincing? Why? Which one did you personally agree with? Why? List some facts and opinions besides those in the viewpoints that have influenced your opinion.

PREFACE: Should the Government Help the Homeless?

The federal government has many programs available to help poor people. One program, Aid to Families with Dependent Children (AFDC), mainly provides assistance to single mothers with children. Other programs, such as Medicaid and Medicare, pay for medical expenses for the poor and elderly. In addition, food stamps help the poor buy food. Whether these programs are enough is debated.

Many advocates for the homeless believe these programs are not enough. They argue that hundreds of thousands of people continue to wander America's cities without places to live. Homeless advocates believe the federal government should provide more assistance. They suggest building more shelters; offering tax breaks to builders who construct low-cost housing; and providing money for job training and counseling.

On the other side, many people believe that the government is already spending too much. They argue that government programs cause poor people to become lazy. Why should the poor go out and get jobs, these people argue, if free government handouts are so easy to get?

The next two viewpoints debate whether the government is spending too much on the poor. Both arguments are quite emotional. As you read, watch for facts and opinions. Do the authors' base their cases mainly on opinion?

The government should do more for the homeless

Editor's Note: The author of this viewpoint states that the government should become more involved in helping the homeless. She suggests several ways the government could help end the serious problem of homelessness.

AP/Wide World Photos

The author lists two ways the government could help the homeless. Does she offer any facts to show that these would definitely help?

Hundreds of thousands, perhaps even millions, of children, adults, and elderly people are homeless in America. What help they receive comes mainly from private charities. But that help is not nearly enough. The U.S. government must become involved in a major effort to save these hapless people.

The United States is the richest country in the world. Its citizens should be thoroughly ashamed to see the panhandlers on the city streets, the men and women sleeping under bridges or wrapped in cardboard boxes and old newspapers in public parks, and the tiny, dirty children who suffer from malnutrition and neglect.

It is time for the attitudes of government to change. No person in this rich country should be allowed to be without food and shelter.

The government could help in many ways. Here are a few of them:

- It could provide money for shelter for the homeless. "Shelter" should include short-term emergency shelter for those who suddenly find themselves without resources. Battered women, young runaways, and adults who suddenly lose homes or jobs are a few of the people who need this kind of shelter. These, like many of the homeless, are not premanently so; many need help on only a short-term basis.

- The government should also provide money for longer-term temporary housing. Some people need help for several weeks or months to get back on their feet. A family's financial resources can be completely wiped out by high medical bills, loss of a job, or loss of their home to fire or flood. With some help, these people can get back to independent existence within a few months.

- The government should provide permanent low-cost housing for those who can expect to be in need of help for many months or even years. These people might include single parents, poorly educated people who can find only minimum-wage work, and people who are partially mentally or physically disabled. This housing should be decent, clean, and kept in good condition.

- The government could provide more money for AFDC (Aid to Families with Dependent Children) and other welfare programs. Presently, the aid received by poor families barely covers monthly rent, much less food and clothing. Peter Rossi is a professor of sociology at the University of Massachusetts in Amherst. He says that in 1985, the average AFDC payment was $325 a month. Anyone who searches the want-ads will see that in many communities, even a one-room apartment costs more than this.

Peter Rossi states a fact—that AFDC payments for 1985 were $325 per month. Find out if this is a fact today. In your city, is that amount enough to provide a family with a home and food?

All of these types of help cost money. But it is time the government and its citizens seriously reconsider the way the country's money is being spent. The cost of a single ICBM (intercontinental ballistic missile), for example, could pay for shelter for many hundreds of homeless people for a year. If the government helped a homeless person for a year, that person might become an independent and tax-paying citizen. This is a much better investment than missiles are.

Should the government give more help to the homeless?

What seems to be the author's main reason for wanting more help for the homeless? Does she use more facts or more opinions to support her argument?

The government is doing enough for the homeless

Editor's Note: The author of this viewpoint believes that it would be a mistake for the federal government to become more involved in helping the homeless. This would only create more red tape and more parasites on society.

Is the statement beginning "It seems to me..." a fact or an opinion? How do you know?

What is the main idea of this paragraph? What facts help support this idea?

Is the last sentence in this paragraph a fact or an opinion?

The government is giving the homeless enough help. It should not provide more. Government programs make people dependent on them, turning them into parasites.

At present, the homeless can receive help from the federal government. They can get welfare money and food stamps, for example. Many state and local government programs also give the homeless shelter, food, and training for jobs. It seems to me that being homeless is not such a bad deal for these people. Unfortunately, it is not such a good deal for the rest of us.

All of this government help leads to more dependence on the part of the homeless. To see what these kinds of programs do, look at what has happened because of government welfare programs. Today we have families that have existed on welfare for several generations. These family members have never held jobs for any period of time; they have poor educations; they have not learned to be responsible for themselves. And as long as they have Uncle Sam to take care of them, many never will learn.

Can a Government Program Help All of These Homeless People?

Poor man   Handicapped   Mother and Child   Alcoholic/Druggie

Under our system of government, people who need help are entitled to it. Unfortunately, some people learn from the day they are born that they do not have to help themselves. If they are poor, the government will take care of them. This is true even if they do not make any effort to help themselves. Now, these people may not live well by middle-class standards, but they do live. Many of them have luxuries such as televisions even if they live in crowded, dirty apartments. The worst part is that these people grow up believing they are victims of society who must be cared for.

We can expect this kind of attitude from the homeless if the government becomes heavily involved in programs to help them. Mike Elias is a former homeless person who runs a Los Angeles shelter. He says, "I've got to brainwash [people who come from other shelters] to let them know that, hey, you can stand on your own two feet; you don't have to be standing around going from church to church, agency to agency, getting handouts."

Elias has the right attitude. C. Brandon Crocker is a financial planner in San Diego, California. He agrees. He says, "We have to treat the homeless as responsible human beings who can change their situation, not as helpless victims who cannot be expected to help themselves." The more the government tries to help and protect these people from helping themselves, the poorer it will make them.

Is Crocker's statement a fact or an opinion?

In conclusion: The government already provides help to the homeless; additional government involvement will only lead to more problems.

Does government help breed parasites?

The author of Viewpoint 4 says that if the government gives more help, the homeless will become parasites on society. What facts does she use to support this argument? Do you agree with her?

Which Viewpoint, 3 or 4, do you more agree with? List two facts that helped you decide.

Distinguishing Between Fact and Opinion

The following sentences are based on information contained in the readings. Write *F* beside any statement you believe is a fact, or something that can be proven to be true. Mark *O* beside any statement you believe is an opinion, or what one person believes to be true.

EXAMPLE: The average 1985 AFDC payment was $325 per month.

ANSWER: Fact: This statement could be proven by calling the library or looking at government reports for 1985.

Answer

1. One study by the Urban Institute shows that there are about 600,000 homeless people in the U.S.   _____

2. Shelter workers say that some homeless people are homeless for only a few weeks.   _____

3. Homelessness is a very serious problem.   _____

4. The government should provide more low-cost housing.   _____

5. Citizens of the "land of opportunity" should be ashamed to see so many homeless people in their country.   _____

6. Homeless people "live" in cars, under bridges, and on the street.   _____

7. Temporary homeless shelters often take in battered women and young runaways.   _____

8. The government is giving the homeless enough help.   _____

9. Government welfare programs are not really helpful because they create dependent people.   _____

10. Recent counts of homeless people show the numbers are going down.   _____

3

PREFACE: How Should Society Treat the Homeless?

Whether or not the homeless are deserving of society's compassion and help is a frequent topic of debate. Many people believe that in America, "the land of opportunity," everyone who wants to can succeed. These people tend to believe that those who cannot make a decent living—those who are homeless, for example—are just not trying hard enough. They do not work hard enough. They do not save their money. They are careless. In addition, their failures create problems for the rest of society. They are a financial burden, and by their presence, they destroy normal community life.

Others, however, believe that many homeless are victims of circumstances beyond their control. They believe they are people who lose their jobs because of company layoffs, lose their homes because of floods and fires, or lose control of their finances because of major medical bills. The people on this side of the issue believe that the homeless deserve society's help. They say that with assistance many of the homeless will regain control of their lives and become contributing members of society.

The authors of the following two viewpoints present their ideas about what society's attitude toward the homeless should be. As you read the viewpoints, look for facts and opinions.

Some people believe the homeless are a bunch of lazy, antisocial misfits who need a good swift kick. But if we look carefully at the makeup of the homeless population, we see that this is not true. The vast majority of the homeless deserve our sympathy and our help.

Is the first sentence a fact or an opinion?

James D. Wright is a professor of sociology at Tulane University in New Orleans. He did a detailed analysis of the homeless. He described his conclusions in an article called "Address Unknown: Homelessness in Contemporary America." It was published in the September/October 1989 issue of *Society* magazine. Professor Wright claims that, if homeless people were looked at objectively, only about one in twenty could be considered lazy, shiftless, and undeserving of help.

Instead, Wright found that many people are only temporarily homeless. Society would lose very little and could gain a lot by helping these people.

Other, longer-term homeless are clearly victims of circumstances they cannot control. Professor Wright states that about 15 percent of the homeless population are children. Many of these children have been abused or abandoned. Others come from families in which both parents are out of work. Clearly, society has a responsibility to help these children in every possible way.

Is the last sentence of this paragraph a fact or an opinion? Does the author provide any support for the statement?

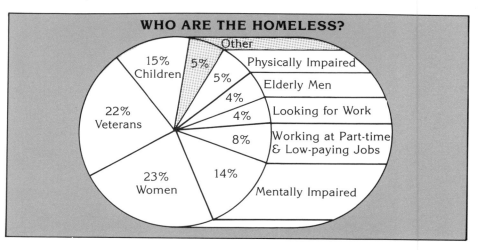

WHO ARE THE HOMELESS?

15% Children
5% Other
5% Physically Impaired
4% Elderly Men
4% Looking for Work
8% Working at Part-time & Low-paying Jobs
14% Mentally Impaired
22% Veterans
23% Women

Another 23 percent of the homeless are women, says Professor Wright. Most of them have children who are dependent on them. And most of them have poor educations and little job experience. When these women can get jobs, the pay is so small that they can barely provide food for themselves and their children, much less pay for child care and housing. Again, society clearly has a responsibility to help these women. The only way they can escape the desperation of homelessness is with financial aid and educational and job training.

The remaining 62 percent of the homeless are single adult males. These are the people Wright says we should look at closely. They are the ones most often suspected of being lazy bums, capable of supporting themselves but too shiftless or drunk to do so. But is this stereotype factual? Professor Wright's study shows that it is not.

According to Wright's accounting, only eight homeless men out of one hundred could be considered undeserving of society's help. This is about 5 percent, or one in twenty of the total homeless population. Shall we abandon all the homeless just to avoid helping these few?

There is another compelling reason to help the homeless: It benefits society to do so. For every homeless person who is aided in a meaningful way, society receives another contributing member. Many homeless people who receive the right kind of help soon become able to take care of themselves. They get jobs, they pay taxes, and they contribute their skills to society. Every person who is helped to cope is one less who drains society's resources.

What facts does the author use to support the idea that helping the homeless will help society?

Should we be compassionate toward the homeless?

James D. Wright concludes that only one homeless person in twenty may be undeserving of society's help. Is his argument based mostly on facts or opinions? Do you agree with his conclusion? Why or why not?

Society should protect its own interests

Editor's Note: The author of the following viewpoint states that the homeless impose on the rights of other members of society. She sees the population of homeless people as a growing problem that threatens society's security and comfort.

Is this statement about authors a fact or an opinion?

The author says our streets and parks are becoming "occupied territory." Does she offer any facts to support this idea?

The author gives a factual example to support the idea that those who support the homeless are becoming disillusioned. But the example would be more valuable if she named the town so readers could check the accuracy of her statement.

Pick up any book on the homeless and check the index under the letter *C.* You will probably find *compassion* indexed, but not *community rights,* says John Leo. He is the author of an essay called "Homeless Rights, Community Wrongs" in the July 24, 1989, issue of *U.S. News & World Report. Community rights* includes the right to live peacefully and safely in one's own community. Leo says we do not find *community rights* in these books because the authors tend to be overly concerned about the living conditions of homeless people, a small minority in our country. These authors forget that the rest of us have rights, too. And unfortunately, the homeless often infringe upon our rights.

Our streets and parks are becoming occupied territory. When we let one homeless person, or two or three, sleep on our street, soon others join them. In a fairly short time, a park can be completely taken over by people like this. No longer does the average person feel comfortable strolling through the park, or taking children there to play. We have lost our park.

John Leo writes, "[Soon,] every park bench seems to be owned by a permanently curled-up, dozing alcoholic or perhaps a street schizophrenic." Worse, he says, "When the cycle is complete, the community withdraws [and] serious druggies and criminals move in." You then have "what Los Angeles and Washington, D.C., are now calling 'dead parks'."

Some cities, with a surplus of compassionate people, have deliberately turned over certain parks to the homeless. They have asked, "What harm is there in letting these poor people use a public resource?" But even they are becoming disillusioned. One California city, for example, passed an ordinance allowing the homeless to camp in city parks. But after only a short time, irate citizens began working to overturn that ordinance. They were fed up with having lost the right to use their own parks without being constantly confronted by panhandling, drunk, and drugged homeless people.

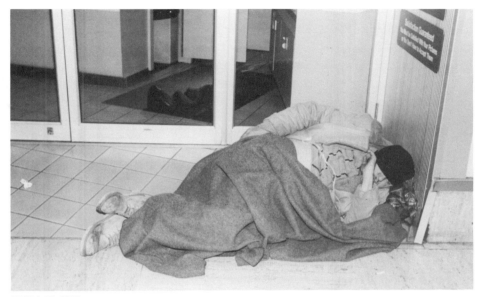
AP/Wide World Photos

In New York City, John Leo says, the homeless established "a permanent shantytown" in Tompkins Square Park. He reports that the inhabitants of this informal slum were poor people, bums, "assorted hustlers, drug dealers, and the mentally ill." This shantytown was filled with the problems you would expect: unsanitary conditions, muggings, theft, and prostitution. The city is trying to regain control of the park. The park department, says Leo, is trying to uphold "the very sensible principle that . . . parks are for recreation, not human habitation."

It is fine to have compassion for the homeless. It is fine to provide shelters and other benefits. But no community should tolerate the violation of its own right to a well-earned, comfortable life in its own streets and public places.

Is this statement about problems in the shantytown a fact or an opinion? How do you know?

Which is more important—community rights or compassion for the homeless?

The author of Viewpoint 6 believes that society's primary concern should be its own interests. List two facts and two opinions she uses to support her view.

Do you agree more with Viewpoint 5 or 6? List two reasons you feel this way. Are your reasons facts or opinions?

Understanding Editorial Cartoons

Throughout this book, you have seen cartoons that illustrate the ideas in the viewpoints. Editorial cartoons are an effective and often humorous way of presenting an opinion on an issue. Cartoonists can place facts as well as opinions in their cartoons.

    The cartoon below deals with homelessness. It is similar to the cartoons that appear in your daily newspaper. Look at the cartoon. What *fact* does the cartoon show? What do you think is the artist's *opinion* about how we should feel toward the homeless?

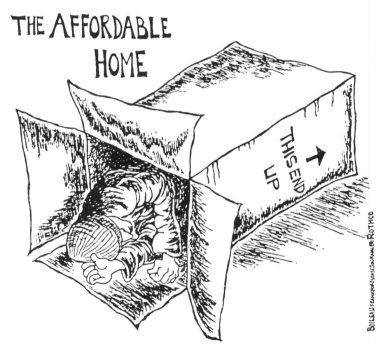

© Boileau/Rothco Cartoons. Reprinted with permission.

    For further practice, look at the editorial cartoons in your daily newspaper. Identify the cartoon's opinions. See if you can find a cartoon that uses fact to back up its statement.

CHAPTER

PREFACE: What Is the Best Way to Help the Homeless?

No matter how people feel about the homeless, they agree that homelessness is a problem. How to solve that problem is a different matter. Probably hundreds of suggestions have been made and programs proposed. Many of these have been tried, but, so far, none has ended homelessness. At one end of the spectrum of solutions is total support of the homeless by providing places for them to live, food, clothing, health care, and various kinds of therapy and counseling. At the other end is the tough, hands-off approach: Let them pull themselves up out of their poverty-stricken lives. While the authors of the following two viewpoints do not advocate such extremes, they do represent two very different places on the spectrum.

As you read these two viewpoints, keep track of the facts and opinions the authors use. Which viewpoint is more fact-based?

Editor's Note: The author of this viewpoint is convinced that the only way to end homelessness is to change the way the homeless think. Rehabilitation programs can help homeless people deal with drug and alcohol abuse, for example. These programs will enable the homeless to once again function as self-supporting members of society.

Does this paragraph contain any facts?

HELPING THE HOMELESS

Living Skills
Self-Esteem
Shelter
Health Care
Job Training
Budgeting Skills

Is the conclusion of this paragraph a fact or an opinion? Do you agree with it?

Many well-meaning people have tried to help the homeless with well-meaning programs. But instead of becoming smaller, the problem of homelessness seems to get bigger each year. But there *are* ways to help the homeless. Unfortunately, these solutions are not quick and easy. They demand time and commitment.

What is needed is long-term rehabilitation programs. These programs must help the homeless learn how to do things they have previously been unable to do. These include budgeting their money, getting proper health care and education, using the social welfare system, and finding suitable and inexpensive housing. The rehabilitation programs must also help the homeless feel better about themselves. They must teach the homeless to have confidence in their own worth, their abilities, and the society they live in. Improving their skills and attitudes is the only way to make a dent in the problem of homelessness.

David Whitman wrote an article in the February 29, 1988, issue of *U.S. News & World Report*. It focused on programs in several cities that seem to be making a real impact. Three of those programs are described here:

- Philadelphia has a program called CORPP (Community Occupational Readiness and Placement Program). It is an intensive, eleven-week job-training program. But it does not focus strictly on the usual job-hunting classroom material such as how to read want ads and how to fill out application forms. The homeless students are asked to think about themselves as persons. What do they want out of life? What skills do they have to offer an employer? What goals do they want to set for themselves? This kind of self-examination can lead to a true commitment to change and a commitment to learn the skills necessary for accomplishment.

- Another Philadelphia program focuses on people with alcohol and drug problems. In most cities, homeless people with chronic chemical abuse problems are occasionally sent to the local detox program for a few days. They are then released onto the street again where they immediately take up their old habits. What is needed instead, say some experts, is "a lot of firm handholding in a transitional setting." Philadelphia's Washington House attempts to do that. It runs a rehabilitation center in a converted garage. Barracks-style housing is provided for thirty-five men for four months after they leave detox. The men who live in Washington House are taught basic skills; they participate in AA (Alcoholics Anonymous); they participate in job counseling. The sponsoring organization's president, Irving Shandler, believes this "on-campus" method is the only way to help these men kick their chronic alcohol and drug problems. And kicking those problems is the only way they can end their homelessness and function in society.

List five facts from this paragraph.

Read the last sentence in this paragraph. It is an opinion. Try to rewrite it so that it is a statement of fact.

- Los Angeles has a unique mental health clinic. Instead of making the clients go to the clinic, the clinic goes to them. A good portion of the homeless have mental or emotional problems or in other ways have difficulty coping with society. It is difficult for these people to to seek needed help. If they do seek it, many cannot keep up the effort of making regular medical and counseling appointments and showing up for them. Thus Dr. Rodger Farr started a drop-in mental health clinic in the poorest part of his city. Dr. Farr also sends out teams of outreach workers to find those who need help but cannot seek it themselves.

None of these programs promise 100-percent success. But all of them do more than stick a bandaid on a problem that requires major surgery. Giving homeless people a little temporary financial aid without teaching them how to find—and keep—a job will make them only temporarily un-homeless. Providing more beds at temporary shelters is also a temporary solution that should be used for emergencies. To end homelessness, what is needed is retraining of these people so that they are able to help themselves.

List one fact from this paragraph.

Do the homeless need rehabilitation?

The author of this viewpoint thinks the homeless have to be trained into new ways of thinking and behaving. Does she offer any evidence that rehabilitation programs work? Do you think she is right?

Editor's Note: The author of this viewpoint argues that rehabilitation programs coddle the homeless, making them even more dependent. She believes they should be offered only sparing, essential help. This would encourage the homeless to want to get back on their own feet, she argues.

A lot of people think that to solve the homeless problem we have to give the homeless all kinds of help: We have to give them comfortable temporary shelters; we have to build comfortable long-term low-income housing; we have to provide education and training; we have to provide therapy. Well, this is not true. These kinds of programs cost taxpayers—the people who work hard for their money and then give a big portion of it back to the government—a lot of money. But worse, these programs do not solve the homelessness problem; they increase it.

Imagine yourself down-and-out. A bad year has forced your employer to fire you; you have been sick and have big medical bills; suddenly you cannot pay your rent. The unimaginable happens: You are evicted. On top of that, you cannot find another job. You panic—what will you do? Finally, in desperation, you take yourself off to your city's homeless shelter, intending to make your stay very brief. But what do you find there? Comfortable furnished rooms, three meals a day, and free counseling to help you cope with your problems. Suddenly, being homeless does not look so bad.

In this paragraph, the author is using a technique called *empathy*. She wants you to empathize with the homeless, to put yourself in their place and feel as they feel.

Unfortunately, this is what a lot of people discover when they become homeless. Many of them can live better with the financial and social services they receive as a homeless person than they could when they were working. Once they discover this, what will motivate them to go out once again, pounding the hard, hot pavement, seeking a job? Why should they work forty hours a week when they can live in comfort while not working at all?

Our nation is known for its welfare system that has bred generations of bums—people who have never worked a day in their lives but live off the hard work of others. If we pamper the homeless, we will be creating more parasites on society.

AP/Wide World Photos

It is unfortunate that there are people in our country without homes. And yes, conscience compels us to help them. But we do not have to provide the comforts that take away their motivation to help themselves.

I believe that every city with a homeless population should have shelters with a limited amount of space. The people in emergency situations should have temporary—very temporary—shelter here. But conditions should not be made so attractive that these people will not want to immediately get back on their own feet. If the shelters are dingy and lack luxuries such as television sets, clients will not want to stay there long. They will go out and seek jobs so they can once again afford their own places with a few comforts. If they cannot get away with sneaking drinks or drugs, they will not want to stay long. They will clean up their acts and rejoin society, or they will go back to the streets where they will be arrested and put away where they belong.

This paragraph is clearly opinionated. What are some of the words and phrases the author uses that show she is not simply making factual observations?

What is the main idea in this paragraph? Do you agree or disagree?

What is the best way to help the homeless?

List four or five of the programs to help the homeless that are suggested in the viewpoints in this book. How many do you think this author would disapprove of for being too coddling? Do you agree with her?

Participate in a class discussion about the homeless. Give your views about the best way to help them.

Using Facts and Opinions

Six topics are listed below. Choose one of them and write two paragraphs about it. Use facts in paragraph one and opinions in paragraph two.

Afterwards, share your paragraphs with two other people. Ask them which paragraph is more effective. Why?

1. The homeless should learn to stand on their own two feet.

2. Our community has a good program to help the homeless.

3. Homelessness is not a serious problem in our community.

4. The best way to help the homeless is _____.

5. Homeless people deserve our help.

6. The main cause of homelessness in our community is _____.

Sample paragraphs

Topic: Our community should provide more shelters for the homeless.

Paragraph 1:

FACTS

Our community should provide more shelters for the homeless. I called the Catholic Charities office in our town and talked to the director. She told me that our town has about nine hundred homeless people every night of the year. Catholic Charities runs two shelters. Together they will only hold about three hundred people. Our city has no other shelters. This means that every night about six hundred people have to find places to sleep.

Paragraph 2:

OPINIONS

Our community should provide more shelters for the homeless. These poor people we see on the street have no warm and secure place to go. I think we would help them and ourselves too if we found places for them to stay. Shelter, a warm supper, and a shower would make them feel better about themselves. These things should also help them be healthier and able to make a better impression when they go to apply for a job. More shelters would help get more homeless people off the streets and back into their own homes.